THE PHILOSOPHY OF AS IF

Fraser Sutherland

BookLand press

TORONTO,CANADA

This book is a work of fiction. Names, characters, places, and incidents are either the product of the author's imagination or are used fictitiously. Any resemblance to actual persons living or dead, events or locales is entirely coincidental. All trademarks are properties of their respective owners.

Bookland Press Inc.
6021 Yonge Street
Suite 1010
Toronto, Ontario M2M 3W2
Canada
www.booklandpress.com

Printed and bound in Canada.

Library and Archives Canada Cataloguing in Publication

Sutherland, Fraser
The philosophy of as if / Fraser Sutherland.
Poems.

ISBN 978-0-9784395-6-9

I. Title.

PS8587.U79P55 2010 C811'.54 C2009-907206-8

I would like a different mind, a different
body, a different life.

Is that too much to ask?

CONTENTS

PART I: BEGGARS WOULD RIDE

PART II: IF WISHES WERE HORSES

PART III: AND ALL SHALL BE REDEEMED

PART I

BEGGARS WOULD RIDE

A PARTY

In darkness my guests dispose themselves
about a rocking table in the middle of my yard,
clumped on collapsing chairs.
Some have dragged out sturdier seats,
and women occupy the back steps,
as though to assert that no one avoids
a passage through the feminine.
With the ceaseless invention so typical of them
my guests have taken candles I've supplied
and stuck them into bottles, no doubt
made other alterations to suit their convenience.
This is one of those parties I am proud to give
in which no one has anything in common.
I lean over the rail to look into the peopled shadow,
the little bonfire bursts of candlelight, and listen
to the distant low agreeable roar,
the nearer sounds of women on the steps
at their tireless plotting, and nod with pleasure
at the world full of these my creatures.

FEEDING

Nights in a life,
even the artificial night of a bar on an afternoon,
door ajar to the light.
I would like to live my life listening
to foreign sounds
and the tastes in my mouth,
foods strange and various.

The child wailing through the wall
keeping you awake
is part of you. It has not been fed.
Feed the child.

City, the smudge we approach,
willing to buy or offer
ourselves. City of cloud
blurring the horizon, what can you give us
we don't possess?
How can you reproach us
for leaving, once we've taken all?

The blanket lifts, and there it is:
the shining domes, gilded palaces,
casbah and fountain.

FRENCH QUARTER, NEW ORLEANS

At 5 a.m., as they go down Toulouse,
a couple halts, the night's last trace.
They kiss, evading morning's noose,
two bodies one in their embrace.

The dinning bars are still
and nothing's left to kill.
On the streets a cleaning crew
sweeps and scours away the mark

of wear and tear as these two do,
a pair of strangers who begin anew,
a brace of stragglers on a dark
slick street off Bourbon, in New Orleans,

and when they lock in shadow I can see
this is important because it seems to be,
and seems important because it is.

BAR GITANOS

The funk gives me a headache and the tape deck spins,
Janis Joplin insisting we take a little piece of her heart.
My shoulders massaged, I'm begged to dance
in the narrows twixt tiny tables and long bar
but I'm not drunk enough, or too drunk with soda scotches
and say I only dance when inspired.
The small neat woman in bangs says,
"I'll try not to take that personally."
At the mike she sang folk country lines she wrote,
a church organ tucked in back of them.
She says I look very much at home. Anyone would
had they come in out of a snowstorm or drank as much as me.
The olive-hued barmaid prowed like a coastguard cutter
spends no little time discussing with a dark woman
the comparative heft and carry of their breasts
and I'm invited to feel my way to judgment
though not of the barmaid's unfortunately who's
serving someone else while I chat with
a slim trim single mother who comes from
a village in the deadly glades of an old country
on the topic of her dysfunctional family,
telling her she's wasting money on a therapist.
She should spend it on the barmaid who knows
everything there is to know about happiness.
The night's intended to launch a young artist,
whose work's mounted on the wall but who in a washroom
mounts or is mounted by the dark woman,
or so she tells me in a taxi with a certain pride,
her story linked to smoky air thick with outcomes.
It could have happened because with gypsies
    anything is possible.

HAPPINESS

In a restaurant's centred patch of sun
she tells of a relationship ending.
I can't guess at what's been done
in the radiance she's sending.

She shows a snap of an island sight,
a house half arbour and half stone,
where she sat in a chrysalis of light,
brown and glistening, herself alone.

She fails to countenance this final break,
all his confusion and her distress,
but now her grin arrives for its own sake,
becoming the emblem of happiness.

The man made her happy on such days,
yet maybe her happiness created all,
as across the tabletop my gaze
absorbs her sunlit face against the wall.

GREEN

A woman told me I had green eyes.
I'd always thought they were muddy blue.

Now I could recognize, acknowledge
jealousy, envy, inexperience,
jetsam-flocked surfaces,
the mixed promise of a broken sky,
a sea after storm that
casts ashore a boyman who,
given his future,
gets up and walks away from me.

CLONING

You never got along with your mother.
nor did she like you.
Clone her, raise her as your daughter,
and make it right this time.

Your father was a monster.
Everyone said he was brutal.
Clone him so you can finally
be brave enough to kick his ass.

You're happily married.
Let not felicity cease.
Clone the two of you
so you may meet and wed again.

If you truly like who you are
but find that life's been unfair
and you wish to gain a second chance...
Clone yourself. Clone yourself.

PROCEDURE

Pushing your portable stanchion
you are conducted
by a large dim stranger
down industrial tunnels
to a bright cheerful bustling room.
You hoist yourself on a trolley
nudging others and
women do painless things to you
Then you are in the dusk
of a narrow terminal
under a low sky
in a long dim line
of others like you,
parked on shelves
ready for shifting.
Female presences glide on
reassuring business.
They have errands.
Then there is nothing.
Then you awake in the light.

GET YOUR STRENGTH FROM SOMEWHERE

Pull your strength from deep inside yourself so it uncoils
slowly like your guts.
Get your strength from someone else but beware in case it
becomes a tug-of-war.
Take your strength cautiously from that many-footed animal,
the crowd.
Put all the strength you get behind the lasso that snares the
world's prayers.
Draw your strength from God hiding in the underbrush.

BURNT RIVER LATE MAY

On my back by the river's edge,
in my ears the river's thunderous ink,
the sun full on my face,
the sun growing stronger and stronger.

MALCOLM, 11, ALMOST HOME

Through the back gate
in the yard he halts,
stands unmoving in the snow,
nerves calmly stretched
like a hilltop fox,
a hunting dog on point
at the still centre
of an elsewhere world.

What does he sniff edged on the cold?
What far-off sound?
The reek of prey? Nearing hoofbeats?

Alert he remains
for poised minutes then
whatever it is,
whatever it was,
he gives it up.
He trudges to the house for lunch,
leaving behind what happens next.

FROM AN IMAGINARY FOLKSONG

I don't ask you to go mad.

Just think of me.
Keep some part of you
forever me.

Remember a slim glass vase,
twin stems intertwined.
Imagine us like that.

I don't ask you to go mad.

Just think of me.
Keep some part of me
forever you.

When you travel
and some mild air reminds you
of one day at the shore

make it us again.
Let that wave
be our wave.

I don't ask you to go mad.

Just think of me.
Keep some part of you
forever me.

Where you're most happy with whomever.
Let me not be him
but hoard a tiny joy for us.

I do not ask a candle
by a photograph
nor a hopeful prayer.

But when the morning or the dying sun
subsides to warm your room
let me have a hand in that.

In our moments
we were too long together.
We should not forget.

I don't ask you to go mad.

Just think of me.
Keep some part of me
forever you.

SCHEHERAZADE

In glade and shade and sun-glanced corridor they walk
and talk. They are practicing the art of delay.
Scheherazade's execution will be postponed
because she's giving the sultan a story that he needs.
The sun tilts into dusk and dark.
As they pass by, each leaf bows, listening.
Neither of them can have enough of stories,
neither wants to make the story end.
Will they ever leave the path they walk?
Will they ever want to?
He inclines his head to hers, his eyes follow
lips that shape a further narrative:
Once the daughter of the town was in the forest with the sultan
and this is what she said to him and what he said to her...

THREE HARMLESS MEN

And so we sit at 3 a.m. in the Kam Kuk Yuen,
this rainy night, John, David, and I,
sharing platters of steamed rice with hacked barbecue,
pork fried rice, the goopy Fuk kin rice.
David and I are deft with chopsticks,
delve into the chili sauce.
John takes his plain with a spoon.
We talk and talk and talk,
discoursing about retired or defeated
prime ministers and presidents,
each pot of tea serving them,
and in between we discuss, at least
do I and David,
the problem of getting John a mate.
John is non-committal,
which may be his problem.
I think he's a good candidate though:
even if he can't cook he's clean.
David reckons that at an unexpected moment
he'll be snagged by someone quite unsuitable.
John's not sure if he's depressed or elated
at the prospect, at least he has a prospect.
David and I seem lost to mates other than our own.
We three are like good women,
hopelessly good.
How the time goes, pot after pot.
The rice is gone, the steamed, the fried, the Fuk kin
and we must go as well, three men
completely harmless.

INSOFAR AS WEATHER

I am somewhere in the mist.
You find me. You take me home.
What happens then? We decide.
I go, you stay. Unsaid.
I'm saying it now, but where you're from
is rain on stone. The message
is in the bottle I drink,
an apology for failure
to incarnate myth, yours or mine.
The actual, which is also myth,
lives moment to day, so far
faraway forgotten as the night we met,
insofar as weather. What kind of night
was it? A night. But afterward,
each of us is different.

THINKING

She sits bent over on a step, writing in a notebook,
dark straight-cut hair half-falling over frown lines,
skirt riding up on neat legs, neither pretty nor plain,
just herself. And I think: We are living
in a steamy flat of hardwood floorboards,
it's a hot summer night, discontent in the air,
though we know it's temporary there's little
to do, see, or talk about. We haven't been married long,
perhaps aren't married at all. I'm slumped in an armchair,
watching as she moves restless, listless, from
one to another room as if wondering she's got
the right apartment for the life she's in.
I don't know this city's name, it could be somewhere else,
but she seems where she ought to be.
And I think: she's not at all like the person with whom I live.
And I think: but this is much the way I'm living now.

AND I PROMISE, IF YOU NEED ME

And I promise, if you need me, I am here.
I will not go to you, except perhaps to lift the phone
for a call brought on by who knows what memory.

Or I'm doing nothing in particular, opening the fridge
in hope of finding lunch when I hear
in the dusty yard a car drive in, it's you.
Though you have had to travel
great distances to see me, underwent
much trouble on the road, what I give you
may not be much relief.
Though I give advice and like to give it
it may not be of use to you.

Or I'll be on holiday, a tourist who
sits on a beach and sips through a straw
when, foot-weary, you trudge down to the surf.
Then after you have your say and I reply

you leave, and though what brought you to me
remains unchanged, we both are changed by what
sent you to me.

Or I'm in my usual tavern,
Tuesday night, drinking beer with the boys,
a girl or two, and suddenly through the fug
your face emerges, raising quizzical looks.
From the rim of my glass I see that you are here.
A few hushed words and I tell my friends,
"Sorry, I have to go."

GOING DOWN

And I am going down into the valley
along the dirt track that flanks the slope.
Trees, bushes, grass grow on either side,
they and the bottomland are green.
The day and land are tropical.
Far off arc the tiny houses of a village
below the point where track meets road
like something snatched from recollection.
The track's not so steep I skid: I keep my equipoise.
Higher up I saw far more than I do now
so I could sit, and look, and take it in.
Now I am going down into the weave.
Always down the jungle road by the muddy river
with the force of dreams awaits the tropictown.

AT THE DELI

My friend and I were sitting in a busy deli north on Bathurst Street. A family sat behind me, recognizable as a grandfather, daughter, and two small grandsons. My friend, a grandfather himself, faced them. He pointed out that the man was in distress. Swarthy, with a big belly, he looked ill. The daughter, blondish with a wide calm face, took her father away from an untouched smoked-meat sandwich, and sat him down near the deli's entrance. She was holding out a paper bag so he could expel phlegm. I went up and asked if I could help get him outside. She said, "I am pleased to accept." I took one arm and she another, and we got him into the corridor. A grandson came up, wondering what was going on. His mother hushed him back to their table. We spread wide the glass door. It was a spring day, and raining. We stood under the awning. My friend settled the bill and brought my coat. I wished the family luck. When we drove away the family was no longer there.

This story could have several outcomes.

Perhaps she took her father to a hospital emergency.

Perhaps he got a little better, she gathered up the boys, and they all went home.

These stories have endings, but the story will never end.

A FICTION

I remember
how you rimmed the moistened lip with salt,
the glass turning in your hand.
That much at least is true,
but from now on you will have to watch
more closely, see
how the words run down.
You have slept as easily as sighs
dissolving, your issuing breath
a hazy mandala.
You have walked in an orchard, picked an apple,
offered it to me.
I could not turn away from that.
Here is the way, the truth, the word:
at last my life is fiction.

PART II

IF WISHES WERE HORSES

BEGINNING

These are days when I would want to begin again
in some stranger-city, to drift into a bar
secretive and self-contained, my whole past
packed inside me like a bomb. An unknown
city, free of personal
associations. To begin again. To flower, each petal
full-looming in the light, until identified
as a common weed and then I
move on. To feel that lonely-aching hotel room
until I come to myself and strangely then
am grasped by others. To find new streets,
cafés, restaurants, and parks, a different soil,
to say, *it's me, I'm here* as indifference breaks
like a grey day's unexpected sun. *You don't know*
about me I'm more than you think.

SELF-CONSUMED

In the red persuasion of stretched skin,
the thudding flesh, we feel
sweat's power on the epidermis
salt and soil and suede. Ambidextrous
double-jointed, febrile as a yogi
we strain to prove a point. That glow
pounds it home. Lips surround the glans
drawing from the succulent bulb
a white flower, or hoping to.

Arms surround ourselves, we are going
deeper, the cave encloses the explorer hardened
for an unspeakable penetration, who
will go plunging on and on
in hope of the more receptive mouth.

DOGS

Why do we like these creatures of habit,
champions of pack order and good government,
anointing their way with messages
and like good administrators never receiving one
without dispatching promptly a reply,
even in dreams vigilant to the rule of law,
liking nothing better than the accustomed round,
yet eager to make the unfamiliar a routine,
happiest when most socialized, demanding I.D.s,
swift to invoke the bite of justice,
convening meetings with agendas, and then
other meetings to discuss what was discussed,
considering the option of interspecies pursuit,
pleased that we can join them on the path
of territorial imperatives and heads-up diplomacy,
or is it that they, like we, are hunter-gatherers
so that we share their indiscriminate appetites
and the immoderate joys of snorting air,
or that they're sorry to see us go and glad to see us back,
that we stop and start to their tails' wigwag,
that we tune our ears to the pitch of the ears
of these whose eyes view the world in shades of grey
but whose noses will not rest...

MORALITY

Still to be gentle, still to be good
in the matrix of morality
my lingam, your yoni.

Alyssum, Albinoni of flowers
grave, alabaster,
reposeful in curvature, immaculate,
allegorical, seeking analogues.
Assuming we have its measure
let us go easily to its alter
ego made pliable
to an ancient devotion.

LOYALTY TO AN OLD IDEA

I.

Beyond particulate, she waits,
my loyalty to an old idea.
These almond eyes are the slots of chance.

This soul a dredge drawing up sediment
of dreams, racial memory, ancestors
who may have been Chinese,
woven fingers on a jar,
my fingers now reach across centuries
and clutch the note, bar, phrase,
as dolphins flourish, a blue flute beyond my depth.

Let me hold, like a heavy bunch of lilacs,
the evening's colour.
If a flower had a will it might renew its petal
or ink, its stain.
And this, anonymously lovely
might be mine.

II.

The only way to possess wholly
is with the eyes.
It's free. Complete.

There are skins beneath skins.
Go deeply
into the retina, into the body.

Crossing the street, crow's wing.
Another desire, quoting
the slim alphabetic fingers.

Into this tranced collation
I blunder; arbitrarily,
a braided waitress
in an Avenida restaurant
whose smile is precious metal Mexico.

III.

Though you were years, a continent away,
though these lines are written
in a language you cannot understand
they're written for you, a moment's utterance
when fingers sang upon my arm, their message
distress and fear and belief in me. Your eyes and hair
black as the night from which we came,
into which we went.
Days will come when my heart will stop
for an instant to see her strip tissue
to show the shining wound.
Your sisters also wait in single file, just around
the corner. Our lines cross,
enigmatic signals travel. I send
scratch-marks, butterfingered semaphores
out into the night in search of you.

IV.

At the back of a book she has written her name
in ideograms, on a scrap of paper
her telephone number. A bobby pin, a hair
in the bath, remind me that
she has been here, traces of a ruined civilization
persuading me one night was long enough
to include the now in which I perish,
a stencil upon time, as museum walls
are crowded with the wary living.

My days are huddled to her
she has left her text on me,
the macrocosmic particle whose finger traces
silhouette-facsimile, in air the very likeness.
Someday a sign will be enough, a mark, a stroke
calligraphic. I will not suffer,
will not have to live that startled joy
a first slow entry as statues come into their being.
I will not have to taste, be lonely or ecstatic,
will not have to catch the train
or wait and welcome home a friend.
I will not have to tend the garden
but find a forest in a weave of paper,
storms in the still bottle. I will be satisfied.
One stroke, a sign, a mark across the white page
will be enough. As in a Chinese wall-painting
someday like those flamingos I will fly
straight to the hieroglyphic
as clouds trail the branch.

PATIENCE

The Asian girl in the quilted jacket is sitting near
the door of the Wok & Noodle, which admits icy drafts.
She noncommittally waits for her order to arrive.
She is wearing thick running shoes. Across the street
a narrow car comes down a wide alley of buckled asphalt
and the air whirls with a crystal conspiracy.
Someone hurries by the window, a phone frozen to his ear.
Everyone hurries in this subzero
yet there are places in this country that assuredly are colder,
in snowdrifts, by an iceberg, by a glacier.
Eventually her order comes: a bowl of white rice
and a sizzling platter cloaked with a paper napkin.
Steam rises from it like a fumarole.
She waits for it to lessen, cautiously peels back the paper,
begins to mix the meat into rice, begins to eat.
She wears running shoes. As if to train.

I WOULD LIKE TO WITH YOU

I would like to have a dozen lives, each one different.
I would like to live these lives with you.
Aboard a bus, springs half-shot, brakes half-gone, bumping
across a mountain-rimmed plain strewn with boulders,
I would like to lurch with you.
After coats are flung on a bed of a room of a hotel of a city of
a country of a continent I would like to stare at the street
with you.
At the rail of a pitching channel boat, in troughs, on peaks,
I would like to be seasick with you.
Before and after a drink is drunk, I would like to get drunk
with you.
Within the chambers of our bodies I would like to have a
heart attack with you.
As a cherry tree is planted, as it grows, as cherries ripen on
the sprig, as they burst against the teeth, as sweet arterial
blood fills the mouth, I would like to plant, grow, ripen,
burst, and fill with you.
Inside a country where unknown trees are begging to receive
their names I would like to name them with you.
Yet in that country the animals have names already and all of
them are tame. I would like to make them wild with you.
Without a decent thing to wear, pulling clothes from racks,
I would like to try on something indecent with you.
During the hour after hour they hunt for us around the
corner, down the alley, where we've gone and where we
go, I would like to escape with you.
While in the crowd, each face reflecting the other's loneliness,
I would like to be alone together with you.
On the day when walls topple and the city lifts a flaming
torch and we flee on foot the cinder road away from it,
I would like to look back with you.
When tropical nights guillotine the day, I would like to be
invisible with you.

EXPLANATION

"You see what happens when I try to give him a compliment,"
she retorts to my mutter, rumble, growl.
What I want to hear has the precision of a formula,
accurate words that have no history, a flower praising the eye.
What faith can I have in ribbons, rosettes, medals
dredged from the swamp of all that people say?
Yet it's true I am fishing for a compliment,
though I fail to specify what it is that I require.

TEXTURE

These evenings I pluck hairs from my beard,
dropping them on the cat's head, an effect
of a yarmulke or small thatched wig.
An editor tells me the manuscript I sent
five months ago is "rising to the top".
Yesterday I took this as encouraging.
Today I'm not so sure.
To safeguard data should I buy a tape backup?
Cajole debtors for reimbursement?
My wife wears a Nicoderm patch like a rose tattoo.
I smoke my smokes in the cramped bathroom,
sliding the window open. The butts refuse to flush.
I fish a wet one from the bowl.
I would like to become a cop.
It would give my life some meaning.

THE LEAST PORNOPHILIC OF MEN

One night and then every night
the least pornophilic of men hears it coming
through the bedroom wall of his new apartment,
the sounds of a woman in apparent ecstacy.
Like clockwork she's at it 8:30 to 11:00.
There seems to be no climax,
it just goes on and on.

Then the least pornophilic of men's
hearing it each afternoon,
from 2:00 to 4:00 the same thing,
and it's gotten so he blushes when
he meets his neighbour in the lobby.
He would like to see her male partner
and size up this epitome of stamina.

Of course the least pornophilic of men
assumes it *is* a male.
Nor does it occur to him that
her cries prolonged and punctual
could be induced by artificial means.

The least pornophilic of men
spends more and more time in his bedroom,
trying to read.

GREAT CLIMAXES

Some great climaxes hide in the lint under a bed then tunnel
blindly before seizing a megaphone and shouting in your ear
unlike the climaxes that whisper all the way along and make
so little sound that you're not sure they're there at all.
Some are headlines about earthquakes toppling San Francisco
and blame the San Andreas fault.
Some are distant rumours about something that may not have
happened, to you anyway.
Some tickle your big toe like a private joke
and others shake you off the mattress and the Beaufort Scale.
Some wrap you in a bear hug so all you can make are
smothered cries
but others toast you in an electric blanket one side at a time.
Some climaxes locate themselves deep within the left breast
or earlobe and maintain no communication with the
outside world.
Others happily spelunk and only come out in daylight.
Some are buttons for a doomsday machine that everyone can
find or may be returned to sender, address unknown.
Some are torpedoes aimed from a block away.
Others are depth charges dropped by the neighbour who
lives just above your head.
Some are the sonic booms of an enraged lioness calling quits
to a safari guide and his Land Rover.
Others are dandelions in fluff.
Some are the crack of dominoes.
Others are an ace up your sleeve.
Some are little notes thanking you for a lovely time
and some are novels in which the hero, after surviving many
adventures, gets killed on the last page.
Some have visiting privileges but nothing gets passed across
the plexiglass
but others unexpected outstay their welcome and you have to
seek an excuse to get rid of them.

Some climaxes are 900-numbers that charge $9.95 a minute, $2.95 for each additional minute when you dialled them by mistake in the first place.
Some are self-catering holidays.
Others are cruise ships where you have to tip the help
and others you yell "Help!" at until the firemen come storming through windows, break up furniture, and tell you to rise from the floor on which you've pressed your face to conserve oxygen.
Some are Masonic signs.
Some are wigwag semaphores.
Some climaxes are endless and are packed in paper bags to take to work.
Others are Scheherazades scribbling *To be continued* on your thighs.
Some great climaxes go on and on in installments and others hardly know where to begin, in fact may have begun with a bedtime cup of cocoa or a story about the Three Bears.
Great climaxes you want to take out a patent on.
Great climaxes you want to tell your friends about but probably won't because who knows whether they're just your imagination or a floater in your eye or something you once inexplicably heard through a wall.

REPLIES TO A LITTLE GIRL IN THE BACK SEAT OF A CAR THAT DRAWS UP BESIDE ME AT A BUS STOP ON A CHILLY NIGHT IN MARCH WHOSE SMILING MOTHER CALLS OUT, "SHE THINKS YOU'RE SANTA CLAUS!"

Withhold your comments should advancing years cause *you* to grow a beard of snowy white.

Allow me to join you in the back seat.

You neglected to note the absence of my reindeer. Nor was there any chimney in evidence. Are you going blind?

Since you have made public the content of your inmost thoughts, did you think to add that I am in fact a fine figure of a man?

Before you tuck your little head tonight into your downy pillow say a small prayer for me.

Has not your mother warned you not to accept candy from a stranger?

It must be tedious to place every time a glass of milk and saucer of cookies on the kitchen table awaiting my descent.

And I think you're just about the nicest little girl I've ever met.

You might assume the cardboard box cradled in my hands contains goodies for the likes of you. Actually, it contains an empty casserole.

Is it your mother's pleasant custom to accost in this fashion a person she does not know?

Farewell until the night I once more shake my hoary locks at you.

Sorry to disappoint you. It's too early for me.

THE ADJECTIVE GAME

After the turkey comes The Adjective Game.
Adjectives will be slotted into
blanks in a prepared script, each paired
with the name of someone in the family.
The regretted absent will receive a copy later.
So, crowded in the living-room, one by one we provide
(the littlest need prompting) adjectives
till all the blanks are filled by a tall thin man
who then reads aloud our story. To laughter,
sometimes forced, we hear of the *pompous W*, the *nubile X*,
the *antediluvian Y*, the *rigid Z*, or as
it may be the e*rudite W*, the *adamant X*,
the *Machiavellian Y*, the *winsome Z*. All
are us, all the above is true, ah,
we cannot tell since this is a family,
dissolving in blood the true or false,
blood bound with others, family overarching all.
But how long can we persist in being family?
When do degrees of separation part us as
matriarchs and patriarchs fade or vanish
and the others age, procreate, grow, or marry?
How long before we find ourselves in a
strange living-room surrounded by unfamiliars
and why am I here and what was your name again?
Yet for decades we have played The Adjective Game,
plucking from the random air exactly who we are.

FROM A HOSPITAL BED

If I push you away
do not think that I reject your love,
or your being seen to love.
What I resist is your—anyone's—power
to make me another,
at the moment someone shown to be in need,
who must display
the allegory of suffering.
Since, in my hurting, I hurt you,
forgive me.
This is all I have left, my body,
its control or lack of it.
Do not admit from me a frail surrender.

I DAILY THINK OF THOSE

who are not famous
and will never be.
They live, they work, they die,
request no premature commemoration,
no answer from the present or beyond.
They see sun and night,
they sleep and wake.
What's added is extra.
Mortal Jesus asked, before they lifted him,
if he might live another day as one of them.

PUNCH

The other day on the sidewalk
a stranger punched me in the mouth.
I never found out why —
I wasn't talking on a cellphone.
Maybe it was an *acte gratuit*
or a rage against the universe
or he didn't like the way I looked
or he got up on the wrong side of the bed
or he didn't have a bed
or from undifferentiated malignity.

Many times I wanted to punch a stranger
and couldn't have said why.
No stranger punched me.
None of this happened.

THE POEM

The poem is tired of being abused.
In the old days it was an oscilloscope
registering the curve of moods.
After a while it wearied of
rehashing childhood illnesses
adolescent lusts, adult idiocies.

The poem is out of its mind
trying to be a tree,
a tragedy, a true confession.
It wishes the poet had more legitimate
means to relieve his mind,
less wasteful ways of exacting revenge.

The poem in point of fact cannot stomach
any longer being *used*,
used as a crutch, a wailing wall, a
sounding board, hollow vessel
into which the poet pours
hopes and tears and fears.

The poem is just so extremely vexed
at being twinned to the poet,
irritated with his heavy smoking,
his gluttony, envy, and self-disgust
and suspects that in these very lines
he's trying to sneak himself in again.

The poem finds life as the poet leads it
inexpressibly tedious.
The poem wants out.
The poem would like to live alone,
take light lunches,
watch what the wind does to grasses.

IMMORTALITY

Surely of all artistic motives the reach for immortality is the most vainglorious. Even if it is never explicit, the artist assumes that what he's doing has permanent value. At the very least he undertakes an existential leap of belief, matching what has often been a loss of face. He wants to conserve and preserve. He has the metaphysical faith that a future for his work exists. Until the work is remembered or forgotten, he will sit on his back stoop watching between a neighbour's garage roof and the trunk of a Manitoba maple the stately transit of 1, 2, 3, 4 teenage raccoons.

PART III

AND ALL SHALL BE REDEEMED

AND ALL SHALL BE REDEEMED

and we shall avoid conflation of what is with what ought to
be, and our subtractions shall add up, amounting to less
and more than we thought

and assumptions and illusions shall take on surprising utility

and an eye for an eye shall see more

and the unique shall refresh the commonplace

and personal preferences shall rehearse categorical
imperatives

and our unctuous editorials and simpering think pieces shall
be reread

and the pornography of grief shall bust a gut

and gambrel, gable, hip, and mansard shall cause roofers to
purse their lips

and each passing shall find the same cleared place for access
and a view

and army ants and army worms shall march, devouring crops
gladly devoured

and targets shall be arrows, and arrow-slits picture windows

and unaffrighted thrills shall attend torched ghettos, and cow
patties and banana peels trail our confident steps

and the hammer — ball-peen, sledge, claw, and tack — shall
find its target, and the nail receive it gratefully

and comedy and tragedy shall retire as roadies emeritus

and a ball shall be a base, a basket, a foot, a hand

and the cold cat warming his bum on the dusty rusty
bathroom grate shall be warm in the end

and the useless shall be harmless, and heedless volcanoes
shall have more reason to erupt, knowing they can do it
harmlessly

and ley lines shall be rescored for didgeridoo

and altar-rails shall kneel before us, and the confessional shed
tears of remorse

and mute pictures shall rewrite captions

and lost possibilities shall be regaled by the actual, and lost
persons shall be found just around the corner, window-
shopping or playing with a dog

and straitjackets shall be lifejackets, and mad people less
sincere

and twins shall become one, or else quite separate, and you
and all around you shall be more than you

and dentist chairs shall be basket chairs, bucket seats, or
bubble baths

and winter-darkened branches shall be algebra, and calculus
dories riding at a dock

and first attraction shall be final attention, and elective
affinities arrange marriages

and the oily matter in finger bowls shall be a subtle rainbow

and ribald jokes of the actual shall entertain dismissed
possibilities

and dyspeptic zones shall be rezoned antacid, and carbon
footprints antioxidants

and wolf spiders shall be content carpenters of webs

and television anchors shall be anchorites, their studios a
hermitage

and speed traps shall be the go in crosswalks, fast lanes slow
fastbacks, and the rabbits in fables outrun complacent
turtles

and click beetles shall be cork tiles, and bedbugs harbingers of
rest

and drop curtains shall be jump seats

and we shall escape being selflessly dedicated to the
discomfort of others

and on the airfield, beyond airfights, below airbursts, airlifts
shall land

and vampires shall receive blood transfusions, and zombies
    obey curfews

and oilfield booms shall bloom oleaginous marigolds, and
    diamond drills condense into dew points

and the hacksaw and bucksaw shall ride across every knot,
    and our hitches, splices, and knots shall hold

and totem poles shall build townhouses, and trailer parks
    tempt timberlines

and treadmills and flywheels shall cage their revolutions

and overdue amends shall caress the waiting anvil

and self-important gravitons shall cleave to the carriage
    of light, and cyclotrons shall bypass colliders, an atomic
    angioplasty

and the body, this clunky machine, shall mesh our motions in
    the air

and messengers shall be commended, their messages shot
    instead

and the shibboleth subtexts of constitutions shall murmur
    passwords

and mortars shall grind pestles

and he shall be contagious and she shall be infectious, and
    both shall laugh

and we shall glide without stepping off the promontory on
which we stand

and the turnings of counterfactuals shall be trailers for an
alternative multiverse

and deceits shall be dabbling upending ducks in a shallow
stream

and puns shall disclose their camouflaged identities: patients
grant patience, crepe and suede take naps, the hours ours,
gophers gofers, the eyes to have it, to write right, and one
shall have won

and , shall be *!*

and we shall recombine disparate elements to recover what
was lost, given, or paid

and the glasswort shall donate its ash to the tinkling pavane
of a champagne glass half-empty and half-full

and committees shall redraw camels

and worker bees shall forego class envy and drones penis
envy

and conspiracy theories and utopias shall be sighing
denouements

and selfish genes, the elves in selves, shall personalize
medicine

and hope chests shall invigorate horse latitudes

and the expensive advice we dispense we shall accept

and the lump of fear in the throat, the waiting for news bad or
belligerent, shall dissolve

and mourning doves shall end their infatuation with
monotony

and feedback shall be feedbags, and flagstones flowcharts

and ditchwater shall drain fever, and failed harvests heap
plates for the hungry

and the courageous shall find avatars in the cowardly

and designated drivers shall flag down designated drunks

and male penguins shall entrust eggs to blizzards, ideal
incubators

and the centrifugal shall spiral from the periphery, the
centripetal from the centre

and duelling dualisms shall flick the on/off switch

and variations shall be themes augmenting incremental
diminishments

and randomness shall rhyme with synchronicity, and we shall
be free to be predestined

and friends shall recruit friends without requiring mutual
enemies or the halos of enmity

and every act shall be the right thing to do at the time, and
realia shall learn from us, our show its tell

and men, women, boys, girls turned into rubble by
earthwake, made cinders by fire, shall be intact in the
instant just before, tsunamis trial balances, and aftershocks
mildly ironic afterthoughts

and boddhisattvas and garden gnomes shall chat over drinks
on the patio

and animals shall be happily reassigned in their pack and
pecking orders, and the fly agaric, the liver fluke, the
conger eel, who could not help being what they were,
shall persevere in their unfettered pride of being

and oft-iterated lousiness shall hear the hurrying footfalls of
providence

and the princess with her lean hound and attentive unicorn
shall step out of the tapestry's living wall

and the shudderful instants in which you could have been
killed, had there come another second, another fraction
of an inch, shall coalesce into one space, and a world
shall whistle through it

and we shall step in the same river twice without getting wet

and earth and stones in their growth and change shall be
reclaimed, and ringed planets so beautifully pointless shall
spin undropped hula hoops, and for the rocks and gas of
the universe awaiting their chance, their chance will come

and if effort is x, then entropy and inertia shall be y

and concave shall morph into convex, angles of refraction into
angles of reflection

and to ask for life to have meaning shall be a category mistake

and vicarious thrills on jittery screens shall be redeployed as
crowd-scene extras muttering "rutabaga, rutabaga"

and back benches and kitchen cabinets shall be ventilated of
smoke, and bagmen shall roam the badlands, reaping
slush-fund hoodoos

and misery shall be less than edifying and spiritual blackmail
shall give kickbacks to morality

and mobiles shall conduct lightning, point to the washroom,
or signal a change in the weather

and comfort shall seem the second guesses of the primitive

and gurneys shall be chaises longes, hospitals liveweight,
and medevacs solariums

and broken shells shall make savoury omelettes

and the & of ♂ & ♀, ♂ & ♂, ♀ & ♀ shall be ∞

and antimatter shall settle down matter, and quarks shall be
verified

and a spoonful of medicine shall make the sugar go down

and we shall reconvene consensus with a quorum of one

and pot shards from middens shall reshape mosaics'
    curvature

and in the best moments of raptors, predators on the breeze,
    the leopard leaping, the hawk swooping, the shark
    homing, the cat, sleek in stalking, shall find in the tail-up
    squirrel its reflection, each prey holding the unanxious
    moment quivering, a rabbit, head-up, looking around

and hypochondriacs shall be gratified by what was wrong
    with them

and virtue shall reap more than one reward

and we shall reverse wrongdoing as the last best act of
    imagination

and finches shall knot, nightingales bed, toads exalt, snakes
    charm, starlings watch, larks skein, and geese murmur

and against shall be for, and from shall be to

and the energy field of ghosts shall fray

and to back out of a closet shall be how we re-enter a room

and the spin cycle of cyclone and anticyclone shall disappear
    inside each other's spirals

and omnipresence shall take in one thing at a time, and
    meerkats drink in the sights

and seas shall be regained in desert gusts, and marshes march
    on mountains, their burros in command

and consequences shall step back to the lowest rung of the
propped stepladder

and egos with names or bundles of sensations, or events
happening to us, shall split the difference, and substance
entities remember who they were

and structure shall cross-hatch texture

and hedonists shall find orgasms in the annulment of desires,
and hormones regulate fearless pleasures

and redistributed grievances shall equate equity with
equivalence, and resources shall be reapportioned without
being called communism, or anything at all

and kangaroo pouches shall house prisoners of conscience,
the viviparous and oviparous trading keys to their
apartments

and good intentions shall pave potholes

and cosmic emblems shall flourish banners of the immanent

and evolution shall be swift, prudent, thrifty, and progressive,
the tailbone and appendix selected for utility

and the anelli and ziti, the cavatatappi and stelline, the
conchiglie and rotelle, the farfalle and fusilli, the garganelli
and lumache, the radiatori, riccioli, and rotelle shall be all
manner of swimming or wriggling creatures returning to
the sea

and the irregular garbage pickup of the superfluous shall
resupply essential services

and zeniths shall reduce nadirs to a level playing field

and waxworks shall melt, and fly-fishermen fling plaster casts
at fingerlings

and comical physiques shall pollinate mutual kindnesses

and positions, ranks, and powers will be reaccessioned in a
vast new library, and a book turn their pages

and night shall wear prescription sunglasses and aubades
herald serenades

and quasars shall be quanta, and magma cool into plasma

and betrayals and guilts shall graze in harmonious packs

and the hanging baskets of squirrel drays shall be crammed
with spring, and the domestic life of the naked mole rat
shall run in prime time

and armless statues shall lift their restored arms in victory

and retimed time and recompressed space shall auger the big
bang, and vacuum refill plenum

and the homeowner who studies the sprinkler on his
suburban lawn shall verify that, even if he and his
household live in interesting times, equanimity shall be
induced without the aid of drugs

and mullahs and church fathers shall seem a bunch of
children, and harping atheists relinquish roles as priests
and ministers of atheism, and physicists, biologists,
and cosmologists become what they were all along:
theologians

and yearning shall earn reward points

and shell craters shall revert to the armistice of ploughed
fields, mudslides smother roadside bombs, and coffee
cups ride atop the roofs of cars on a long highway
undisturbed

and the clockmaker shall reset the clock, the great mistake
shall be redressed, and the unmoved mover's tears shall
dry

and lip-smacking trends shall be cured of whitecoat
syndrome

and shoots and scions shall engender grafts, and rock, rap,
and roots reclaim the rapture of gospel

and items of use shall be usefully fulfilled, the backless mule
worn lightly on the foot, the reins lain lightly on the
mule's back

and isms and ologies shall be flickered grasses on a savannah

and ingress and egress shall be right of way and right of entry

and moas and dodos shall gaze up at passenger pigeons
blotting out the sky, and dinosaurs shall welcome the
asteroid

and the spangled fritillary shall retrace the flight of the
eight-spotted forester, and the regal horned lizard crown
the sulphur-crested cockatoo

and apogees and perigees shall reel in satellites, and our
bodies' influence tow moons, stars, and planets

and the grave plot shall be our rocking cradle, we shall give
birth to our parents' birthrights, stillbirth reborn at the end
of our biographies

and a plucked string shall be both the string and the sound it
makes

and squares and rectangles shall stretch into circles and
ellipses, and attachments expand the circles to which they
were attached

and the immense earth shall reclaim the immense sky, and
big-shouldered mountains stand equal to sunset skies,
specks equal to a windowpane

and names and addresses shall reassign themselves to
grateful recipients, and cheques shall really be in the mail

and exponential windlasses shall power up circuit boards

and souls and bodies shall be each other's shadow puppets,
and star in each other's matinées

and hinterland and metropolis shall reabsorb their populated
solitudes

and the bird cherry shall genuflect to the bird colonel, the bird
colonel shall salute the bird cherry, and the rear admiral
set sail as the white admiral

and doubt shall respell certainty, proof rest on a hypothesis,
and horizon-line explanations meet at the vanishing point
of faith

and emperor and empress shall share the unspoiled spoils of
risen empires, and fallen empires shall be erector sets

and the farmer's footsteps shall stride across fathoms of acre-
feet, and freeze and thaw regain firm footing

and we shall roll in piled unscattered leaves

and causation shall denote causes as nothing to do with them

and hinnies and jennies shall rejuvenate stallions

and past and future shall perch comfortably on a pinpoint,
and flashforwards revisit flashbacks

and quality and quantity shall be fast, cheap, and good

and shoals of mackerels shall swim in mackerel skies

and bacteria and viruses shall be the body's genial hosts for
autoimmunity

and the cherub shall shed light on the seraph

and chainmail and muscle shirts shall dress white-tie at
nudist camps

and familiars astride our shoulders shall have familiars and
shoulders of their own

and distempered decades shall lave their dirty laundry on
watered stones

and the cardinal shall sift the water's surface, the hawk scoop,
the hummingbird catch, the heron heap, the pelican drill,
the mallard tear, the spoonbill crack, the swallow spear,
and the woodpecker gulp

and the coiling stinking smoke from outsized chimneys, the
shallow grave scrabbled in jungle soil, the casual machine-
gun burst in a sylvan glade, the pyramid of skulls, the
neck sawn through, the frozen feet and then the shot hot
to the back of the head, shall be replaced

and banks shall issue socks so account-holders can save silver
dollars under their mattresses, and sand dollars shall be
their carry trade

and museums shall be solid mirrors through which we stroll

and minuscule shall trade spaces with majuscule, and
spindrift diacriticals dance on letterforms

and we shall be spared the smudges and smuts of cleanliness

and claustrophobia shall go spelunking in caves where
agoraphobia cancels vertigo, and cramped burrows shall
be commodious

and the crippled boy splayed across the toilet bowl, whose
teeth rotted and then fell out, and who ended on a rubber
sheet in an old folks' home and had one testicle excised in
the same hospital in which he later died of pneumonia,
and who, lacking merit deserved no grace, he shall forgive
the arrangements for who and what created him

and flowers shall reincarnate sprouting seeds, and forest fires
rain seedlings

and dreams shall strengthen double-blind experiments,
continuous with waking, and we shall regain a focused
drift in reveries

and a loaded word shall lose its stuffing

and secrets shall release the subsonic harmonies of woofer
and tweeter, wow and flutter

and labour shall be surplus value, and the jobs proposed to us
shall be those we keep

and we shall forego swallowing large metallic objects and
biting off our lips and fingertips

and windshield wipers shall swoosh onions' stinging tears

and justice shall throw tantrums of good temper

and fingerprints shall be finger paintings, and palmprints tea
leaves read in china cups

and we shall marvel that what we stared at had been gazing
back at us

and the memory of rapes and murders shall be like the
memory of labour pains or surgery, a memory of a
memory, and we shall forgive that we forget

and we shall be freed from making faces at ourselves

and vectors shall be vents, and vicious circles valves

and elements shall set the periodic table with blank place
cards for phobias, philias, and manias

and electrical storms in the cauliflower brain shall pulse
steadily and gently

and endlessness shall extend the endings of renewal, and
arrivals and departures shall book returns

and victims shall review the parade of monsters in their pride
and greed whose tears shall cleanse victim stigma

and bells shall repeal organized error

and sparrows clumping on the winter branch shall lift their
wings and the apex of a roof, a triangle of snow, shall give
each to the air

and skyscrapers shall spare the sky, and high-rise window
washers polish clouds

and the one-damned-thing-after-another shall be the all-at-once

and contrails shall fly the planes preceding them

and intrinsic elements of closed systems shall endorse
endogamy

and the still surface of the gaping cistern shall be unominous

and infidels shall regenerate the sacral in blasphemy, and
adventitious defilements refurbish rituals

and the talented and the beautiful shall recall the blessing of
being born deformed, and healed childhood shall
revaccinate the genius of prodigies

and floor-sweepers shall board the ark two by two

and suicides shall cultivate the habit of second thoughts

and neurons shall leapfrog the synapses of merit and demerit

and the reason that there is something rather than nothing
shall be that nothing is something

and those who said they loved the world shall love the world

and objects shall be farther than they appear in the rearview
mirror

and dictionaries shall describe things, and encyclopedias
describe words

and the privacy of those who enter bathrooms whose doors
have been left open or unlocked by their occupants shall
be preserved, and the public shall withdraw into the
privacy of shower stalls

and clothes tumbling in the porthole of the dryer shall attain
oracular significance

and love shall shed tickling quotation marks, and form part
of an entirely new emotion flowing from an organ
different from the organ known as heart

and the pranks of timing — the entombed miners are alive,
no, they're dead, no, they're alive — shall punch another
clock

and a shell offered to the ear shall echolocate us to the places
we have been

and we shall donate to ourselves when charity begins to roam

and we shall abide the intolerance of tolerance

and red alerts shall turn a tasteful shade of turquoise

and auctions shall proceed unreserved, capped by our
upraised hands cupping the silence of applause

and the downs and ups of stages, stairs, streams, towns, and
winds shall be the wise in sidewise

and zebras shall remind us of zebra finches

and the drive to wage total war, the wars to bring peace, shall
convert to sheer mere energy

and information, knowledge, and wisdom shall rescind their
sequence, and the needs and wants of hardwired nature
and blank-slate nurture nod

and the goalkeeper behind whose back a disc or sphere spins,
trickles, wobbles into the net shall have company at last

and the old lady with multiple cats shall live among them but
the cats, who never liked her all that much and in fact look
forward to a tasty treat on her demise, shall be free of her,
nor shall they have to tender thanks and, as for the lady,
she will be pleased that other cats have joined her herd

and temples shall dispense with fresh hearts and blood, and
the bloodstains on sacrificial slabs shall vaporize

and impermissible questions shall yield admissible answers

and the bad luck of pigs, who taste good and are blamed for
everything, shall be reversed

and all shall be as it should be and should have been, and all
shall last for eternity at least

and those who know what it will be like, including me, they
shall be wrong

ACKNOWLEDGMENTS

This book takes its title from Hans Vaihinger's *Philosophie des Als Ob* (Berlin, 1911), translated by C. K. Ogden as *The Philosophy of "As If": A System of the Theoretical, Practical and Religious Fictions of Mankind* (New York, 1925.) A few poems, sometimes under a different title or in a different form, first appeared in the collections *Within the Wound, Madwomen, Whitefaces, Peace and War* (with Goran Simić), in the *Globe and Mail* (Toronto), and *Saaheb Ghalam* (Tehran), translated into Farsi by Fereshteh Molavi. My thanks to the editors, publishers, and translator concerned, and to Jennifer Compton, John Robert Colombo, Mary Dalton, Stan Dragland, Geoff Hancock, Shane Neilson, and Elizabeth Spencer for the kind things they said about my work, and for their helpful comments.

ABOUT THE AUTHOR

Fraser Sutherland is a much-travelled Nova Scotian who now lives in Toronto, Ontario. Frequently a reviewer for the *Globe and Mail,* he's published fourteen books, including poetry, short fiction, and nonfiction in Canada and the United States. His work has appeared worldwide in numerous magazines and anthologies in print and online, and has been translated into French, Italian, Albanian, Serbo-Croatian, and Farsi. Having written and edited for many dictionaries in three countries, Fraser Sutherland may be the only Canadian poet who is also a lexicographer.